PLAIN
and
not
so
PLAIN
ACADEMY

A simpler approach to home based schooling

Summer review

of

Third Grade

Basic Skills

This book is for the home educator or anyone looking to improve upon their child's skill sets. It contains multiple lessons and skills that will help reinforce your third graders knowledge before they enter fourth grade. It reviews math concepts, reading concepts, and various grammar lessons.

How do I recommend you do this book? However you feel is comfortable. Let me share with you how I wrote the book and will intend to use it with my children.

On page 7, there is a suggestion on how to keep track of your child's book reading this summer. I would recommend doing this to encourage more reading.

I would then suggest you do three pages of learning per day beginning on page 13.

Included are enough pages to do 67 days of extra work.

I hope you find this resource helpful in your child's academic growth. My intention is to help simplify learning to create a more peaceful, organized, and happy home.

Be blessed,

Amy Maryon

founder and owner of www.plainandnotsoplain.com a simpler lifestyle in our complex world

Reading for the summer months.

Encourage your student to read as many books as they can during these summer months. What if your child doesn't enjoy reading alone? You can choose a variety of read aloud books and read to your child. Set aside a specific time of day to do this so that you do it. On the next page let your child, when they are finished reading, write the title of the book and give it a star rating. Pick up a pack of shiny foil stars and let them put in the box the rating.

☆   I can take it or leave it

☆☆   It's good for a rainy day.

☆☆☆   You have to read this one!

☆☆☆☆ It's one of the best books I've ever read!

BOOK TITLE	RATING

BOOK TITLE	RATING

Get two dice and roll 'em.

Here is a fun way for student's to improve recall of math facts. Have student's roll the dice and add the two numbers. Then starting at the bottom of the recording sheet, have the student color in the correct box depicting the sum rolled. Have student's continue in this same manner until they reach the top of one column. Have them announce which number reached the top first.

0	1	2	3	4	5	6	7	8	9	10	11	12

Synonyms

Synonyms are words that mean the same. Write a word in the box that means about the same as the first word.

above	
afraid	
alike	
angry	
auto	
begin	
below	
big	
buy	
chilly	
considerate	
correct	
cry	
damage	

Fire safety

Share these facts with your student about fire safety.

- If a door is hot to the touch, don't open it. There could be a fire on the other side.
- You should walk, not run, curing a fire. Running causes more oxygen to reach the fire, causing the flames to grow.
- If a room is filled with smoke, crawl under the smoke rather than walk through it. The air near the ground will be cooler and less smoky.
- If your clothes catch on fire, remember to stop, drop and roll.
- Once you are safely outside the house, call 911.
- Cool a burn with cool water for about 20 minutes. Do not apply butter or ointment to a fresh burn, they hold heat.

Today do a fire drill with your child. Discuss ways that you are to exit the home in case of a fire. Have a couple different ways depending upon the scenario. Have a designated meeting place outside so that all family members can be accounted for.

Get two dice and roll 'em.

Here is a fun way for student's to improve recall of math facts. Have student's roll the dice and subtract the two numbers. Then starting at the bottom of the recording sheet, have the student color in the correct box depicting the difference rolled. Have student's continue in this same manner until they reach the top of one column. Have them announce which number reached the top first.

0	1	2	3	4	5	6	7	8	9	10	11	12

Synonyms

Synonyms are words that mean the same. Write a word in the box that means about the same as the first word.

different	
dirty	
drink	
drowsy	
easy	
end	
enemy	
false	
fast	
fight	
find	
fix	
friend	
funny	

Helpful or harmful?

Help your student think about the good and bad qualities of fire. Have student's fill in the following chart completing the sentences and illustrating a picture.

Fire is good because.......	Fire is bad because.......
Fire is good because.......	Fire is bad because.......

Let's fill in the hundreds chart

1									

Synonyms

Synonyms are words that mean the same. Write a word in the box that means about the same as the first word.

glad	
go	
grin	
hard	
healthy	
home	
hot	
incorrect	
intelligent	
jog	
jump	
keep	
late	
look	

What would you do?????

Ask your student the following question:

What would you do if a stranger approached you and said………?

- Would you like some of my candy?
- I've lost my puppy. Can you help me find him?
- I have a special gift for you in my car. Come with me.
- You look just like my favorite grandchild. Do you mind if I take a few pictures of you.
- I can't hear you very well. Come a little closer to me.
- Your parents have been in an accident and I'm here to take you to the hospital to visit them.
- I have your parents on my phone. Come over here they'd like to talk to you.
- Can you help me put these groceries in my vehicle for me?

What would you do if you got lost in the store?

What would you do if someone approached you in the bathroom?

What is something you can do to protect yourself -----always go in pairs.

Stranger safety is something to sit and discuss over with your child/student today.

How many months are there in one year?_____

Name all of the months to your teacher………………………………………..

What number month is your birthday?_____

How many days of the week are there?_____

Write the days of the week?

Synonyms

Synonyms are words that mean the same. Write a word in the box that means about the same as the first word.

loud	
many	
neat	
odd	
rip	
road	
shout	
skinny	
small	
soggy	
story	
stroll	
surprised	
throw	

Interesting inferences

Have students use what they know about the characters to decide how each character might react to the situations below. Answer the following in one to two sentences.

What would the character do…………………………………

If you found a lost dog on the highway?_____

_____

_____

If her best friend ignored her on the playground?_____

_____

_____

For fun on a rainy day?_____

_____

_____

If she found a wallet full of money?_____

_____

_____

Fill in the chart counting by 2s

2									

Count by 5's

5									

Count by 10's

10									

Count by 25's

25			

Antonyms

Antonyms are words that have the opposite meanings. Fill in the following chart with a word that means the opposite of the first word.

above	
add	
alike	
asleep	
backward	
bad	
beautiful	
begin	
believe	
big	
buy	
catch	
clean	
close	

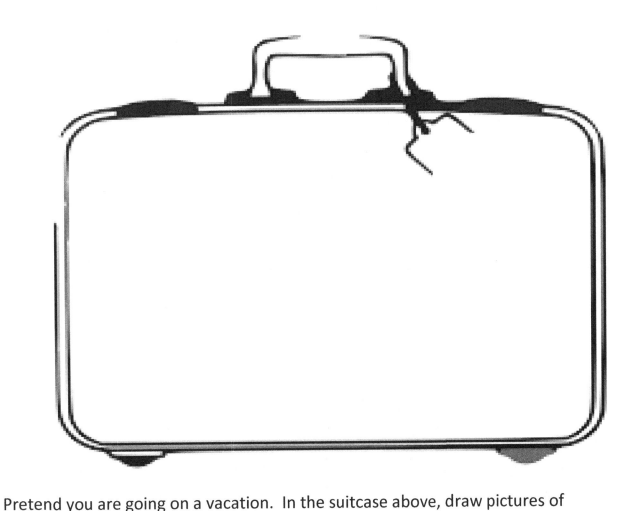

Pretend you are going on a vacation. In the suitcase above, draw pictures of things you would take along with you on your trip. Then write a few lines about the things you would take and where you are going.

_____

_____

_____

_____

_____

_____

_____

_____

Alphabet symmetry. Grab a ruler and place it on the following letters to draw a line of symmetry. Explain to students that a figure is symmetrical if has at least one line of symmetry. A line of symmetry divides the figure into congruent parts, or two parts that are the same size and shape. Some of the letters may not have a line of symmetry.

A   B   C   D

X   Z   M   I

Q   R   S   T

H   K   G   L

Antonyms

Antonyms are words that have the opposite meanings. Fill in the following chart with a word that means the opposite of the first word.

cold	
come	
crooked	
cry	
dangerous	
day	
deep	
destroy	
difficult	
down	
dry	
early	
enemy	
false	

Encourage your child to create a newspaper by filling in the following with fictionist stories.

Weather report

Estimation

Have your student estimate the following answers. Then do the actual measurement and see how close they were.

Activity	Estimated Amount	Actual measurement
How many steps does it take to get to your bedroom		
How long is your table		
How tall is your table		
Grab a handful of small snacks—cereal, crackers, pretzels, etc. How many do you have		
How many cans of food do you have in your food cupboard?		
How many windows do you have in your home?		
How many toothbrushes do you have in your home?		
Stack five books on top of each other. How tall is your stack?		
How many cups do you have in your cupboard		
You choose some things to estimate:		

Antonyms

Antonyms are words that have the opposite meanings. Fill in the following chart with a word that means the opposite of the first word.

fancy	
fast	
fat	
few	
float	
forget	
found	
frown	
generous	
give	
happy	
hard	
healthy	
left	

Use a roll of the die for a capitalization challenge. For some review, instruct your student to write a sentence containing proper nouns. Explain that the number on the die will determine how many capitalized words each sentence must contain.

1

2

3

4

5

6

Artistic measuring

Direct students to draw a house 8 centimeters tall and six centimeters wide, a door three centimeters tall and two centimeters wide. Have them add more detail and color.

Antonyms

Antonyms are words that have the opposite meanings. Fill in the following chart with a word that means the opposite of the first word.

loose	
lose	
mean	
narrow	
noisy	
old	
over	
play	
peace	
polite	
poor	
right	
rough	
save	
short	
sour	
tame	
terrible	
whisper	

Have your student brainstorm a variety of words that are to be capitalized. They can write them in random places on this page. Encourage them to include a variety of proper nouns.

Measuring Me
Find the following measurements on yourself.

Hand	foot
thumb	arm
leg	Shoulder to shoulder
Pointer finger	nose

Have your student read through the following list. If they need to, copy the words on index cards, show them the word, and then let them hop towards you as they get them correct or stand in place and jump or clap their hands. Any activity that increases motor skills can be used.

afternoon
corncob
flagpole
landowner
raincoat
sunrise
airline
cornmeal
flashlight
lifetime
raindrop
sunset
airplane
cowboy
flowerpot
lighthouse
rattlesnake
sunshine
anybody
cowgirl
football
lookout
roadside
sweatband

Have your student brainstorm nouns, verbs, and adjectives associated with summer.

Summer		
nouns	**verbs**	**adjectives**

Draw a picture describing summer

Draw an example of the following shapes and then find an item in your home that matches it.

shape	draw it	household item
circle		
star		
square		
rectangle		
sphere		
cube		
pyramid		
cylinder		

Have your student read through the following list. If they need to, copy the words on index cards, show them the word, and then let them hop towards you as they get them correct or stand in place and jump or clap their hands. Any activity that increases motor skills can be used.

anyone
cupboard
footprint
lunchroom
rowboat
sweatshirt
anything
cupcake
friendship
mailbox
runway
sweetheart
anyway
daybreak
gentleman
mailman
sailboat
swordfish
anywhere
daydream
gingerbread
mealtime
salesman
tablecloth

Have your student list 10 adjectives to describe the following words:

ice cream	kittens	the beach
1	1	1
2	2	2
3	3	3
4	4	4
5	5	5
6	6	6
7	7	7
8	8	8
9	9	9
10	10	10

Reinforce estimation skills by giving some paper clips or other similar items to your student. Provide them with a variety of items to measure. Let them list the item, estimate how long, and then to check the estimation.

Item	Estimation	Actual measurement	Were you correct? yes or no

Have your student read through the following list. If they need to, copy the words on index cards, show them the word, and then let them hop towards you as they get them correct or stand in place and jump or clap their hands. Any activity that increases motor skills can be used.

arrowhead

artwork

ballpark

bareback

barnyard

baseball

basketball

bathrobe

bathroom

bathtub

bedroom

bedspread

bedtime

beehive

birdhouse

birdbath

birthday

blackboard

blacksmith

bluebird

boxcar

breakfast

broomstick

butterball

Create a flip book for your student.

To make a booklet, stack three, 8 ½"x11" sheets of white paper and hold the pages vertically in front of you. Slide the top sheet upward one inch; then repeat the process for the second sheet. Next fold the paper thicknesses forward to create six graduated layers or pages. Staple close to the fold.

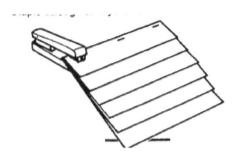

Have your child create their own story.

They can write about what they like to do in the summer.

All about their pet.

What they did on vacation.

Illustrate and add correctly written sentences.

Reinforce graphing skills with a tasty treat. Give each student a snack sized bag of color candies. Have each child sort and graph their candies by color on their graph paper. Then using the corresponding crayon color, have them color one square for each candy of that color. Encourage them to write the total number of each color on the graph. Then challenge the child to add the total number of candies.

Total number of candies_____

Have your student read through the following list. If they need to, copy the words on index cards, show them the word, and then let them hop towards you as they get them correct or stand in place and jump or clap their hands. Any activity that increases motor skills can be used.

buttercup
butterfly
campfire
campground
cannot
cardboard
catbird
catfish
cattail
chalkboard
clothespin
cobweb
copycat
cornbread
doghouse
dollhouse
doorbell
doorknob
doormat
doorway
doughnut
downhill
downstairs
downtown

Copy the following nouns and verbs on pieces of paper. Place them in two piles. Let your child choose one noun and one verb from the pile. NOUNS: mother, dog, park, helicopter, boat. VERBS: planted, jumped, swam, ate, flew. Now have them write a sentence that includes both the noun and the verb. Sentences can be silly.

1

2

3

4

5

Create a pictograph on how many glasses of water are drank each day by people in your family or friends.

Person	Draw the number of glasses drank

Have your student read through the following list. If they need to, copy the words on index cards, show them the word, and then let them hop towards you as they get them correct or stand in place and jump or clap their hands. Any activity that increases motor skills can be used.

driftwood
driveway
drugstore
drumstick
eardrum
earring
earthquake
eggplant
eggshell
evergreen
everybody
everyone
everything
everywhere
eyeball
eyebrow
eyelash
eyelid
farmland
fingernail
firecracker
fire fighter
firefly
fireman

Pop up cards

Students will enjoy illustrating their stories in a pop-up card. Have your student publish their favorite story in a self-made pop-up card.

To make a pop-up card:

1. Fold in half a 9"x12" sheet of white construction paper.
2. Cut two 2-inch slits in the center of the fold about 1 ½ inches apart. Open the card and write a short story near the bottom of it.
3. Illustrate the main character in the story on a three-inch square of construction paper. Cut out the illustration.
4. Pull the narrow strip in the center of the opened card forward and crease it in the opposite direction from the fold. Glue the cutout to the lower half of the strip; then illustrate the inside of the card as desired.
5. Close the card, making sure the strip stays inside.
6. To complete the project, write the title of the store on the outside of the card.

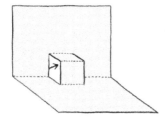

A sample story may include:

One day I was walking in the forest when I met a bear named Susan. We became friends. I took her food and taught her how to dance.

Make a bear and attach it to the square. Color in the background to look like a forest.

Supply your student with three dice. Have them roll the dice and then add up the three numbers. Record them on this page. Then have them roll again and add that amount to the previous number. Keep rolling until they reach 100.

Have your student read through the following list. If they need to, copy the words on index cards, show them the word, and then let them hop towards you as they get them correct or stand in place and jump or clap their hands. Any activity that increases motor skills can by used.

fireplace
firewood
fireworks
fishbowl
fisherman
grandmother
grandfather
grapefruit
grasshopper
greenhouse
groundhog
hairbrush
haircut
halfway
handshake
headache
headband
headfirst
headlight
headline
headrest
headstand
headstrong
heatstroke
highchair
hillside

Have your student grab five items from their room. Now have them give you one fact and one opinion about each item. We are reinforcing fact and opinion. As the teacher you can provide a variety of other fact and opinion examples.

Give your student three dice and have them roll, and then add up the amounts. Take this amount and subtract it from 200. Continue doing this until they reach zero.

Have your student read through the following list. If they need to, copy the words on index cards, show them the word, and then let them hop towards you as they get them correct or stand in place and jump or clap their hands. Any activity that increases motor skills can be used.

homemade
homework
hopscotch
horseback
horsefly
horseshoe
hourglass
houseboat
household
housewife
hubcap
indoor
inside
into
junkyard
keyboard
ladybug
landmark
milkshake
moonbeam
moonlight
moonscape
motorboat
motorcycle
mousetrap
necklace

Summarized stories

Have your student create a shortened version of a chapter book that you have read. Make a book out of construction paper folded in half and stapled. Include 5 pieces of paper. Let them decorate the front with the title and a photo.

Encourage them to write a couple sentences on each page along with an illustration, summarizing the book. Do not use the word "and" more than once on each page.

Write the numbers 0-9 on index cards. Place them facedown on the table. Have your child pick up three cards and quickly place them in order to make the largest number possible. Do this numerous times.

You can then play and have them make the smallest number possible.

You can choose a card and say make a number with these three cards where the "2" is in the tens place. Do this for the other place values.

As they get more confident, you can add thousands to the places.

Have your student read through the following list. If they need to, copy the words on index cards, show them the word, and then let them hop towards you as they get them correct or stand in place and jump or clap their hands. Any activity that increases motor skills can be used.

necktie
newspaper
nighttime
nightcap
nobody
notebook
nothing
outcome
outdoors
outhouse
outline
outside
overall
overcome
overlook
overtime
paintbrush
pancake
patchwork
peacock
peanut
pillowcase
pincushion
playground
pocketbook
policeman

Following directions

Read all of the instructions on this page before beginning. Draw a star in the lower right hand side of this page. Draw a large circle in the center. Make a line under the circle. Write your name above the circle. Make a rectangle in the lower left hand side of the page. Draw a heart within the circle. Number down the left hand side of the page 1-10.   Now that you have read the directions and have not written anything, you can smile because you followed the first sentence☺

Practice writing numerals

In the following boxes, write all of the possible numbers that you can make with the numbers given.

7 2 1	3 5 8
9 7 5 1	**6 4 8 2**

Now circle the greatest numbers that you created within each box. Make a square around the smallest numbers that you created within each box.

Have your student read through the following list. If they need to, copy the words on index cards, show them the word, and then let them hop towards you as they get them correct or stand in place and jump or clap their hands. Any activity that increases motor skills can be used.

popcorn
postman
quarterback
railroad
rainbow
scarecrow
schoolhouse
schoolyard
scrapbook
seahorse
seashore
seesaw
shipwreck
shoebox
sidewalk
skateboard
smokestack
snowball
snowflake
snowman
somebody
somebody
someone
something
somewhere
spaceship

Illustrate and write three sentences about what you are enjoying about summer vacation.

Circle the correct operation to perform the following story problems.

Autumn and Madelyn went to the beach and found some pretty shells. Autumn found five green ones and Madelyn found three red ones. How many seashells did they find altogether at the beach?

How would they solve this story problem?   Addition +   or Subtraction –

Jentzen had 10 toy cars. Stephen came along and took 4 to play with. How many does Jentzen have now?

How would they solve this story problem?   Addition +   or Subtraction –

Jadyn wanted to bake some cookies for her class. She already had 15 chocolate chip cookies made but her class has 20 students. How many more cookies does she need to bake to have enough for her class?

How would they solve this story problem?   Addition +   or Subtraction –

Brooklyn drank five glasses of water in the morning and three in the afternoon. Later that evening she has 2 more. How many glasses of water did Brooklyn drink today?

How would they solve this story problem?   Addition +   or Subtraction –

I have ten children and I want them all to have six pairs of socks each. How do I figure out how many socks to buy?

I would subtract the numbers   I would multiply the numbers

Have your student read through the following list. If they need to, copy the words on index cards, show them the word, and then let them hop towards you as they get them correct or stand in place and jump or clap their hands. Any activity that increases motor skills can be used.

springtime
stagecoach
stairway
starfish
starlight
steamroller
stopwatch
storeroom
storybook
strawberry
suitcase
summertime
sunburn
Sunday
sundown
sunflower
sunlight
yourself
worthwhile
woodland
without
within
wintertime
windshield
windmill
wildlife

Menu activities

Choose one of the following lunch meals for your child to answer the following questions with.

Pizza with meat Green beans Applesauce Milk	Sloppy joes French fries Corn Pear slices milk	Peanut butter and jelly sandwich Banana Carrot sticks milk

Name an item from each food group: Dairy_____

Fruits and vegetables_____

Grains_____

Meat/beans/protein_____

Alphabetize the food items

1. _____

2. _____

3. _____

4. _____

5. _____

Count the number of syllables in each word. Write the number next to each item in the list above.

Name the ingredients in each item.

Practice addition with a deck of cards.

Give your child the number cards in a deck.

Let them flip up two cards and then add the amounts together. Fill in the chart below with the sum they get. When they reach the top, the game ends.

1	2	3	4	5	6	7	8	9	10	11	12	13	14	15	16	17	18	19	20

Have your student read through the following list. If they need to, copy the words on index cards, show them the word, and then let them hop towards you as they get them correct or stand in place and jump or clap their hands. Any activity that increases motor skills can be used.

taillight
teacup
teamwork
teapot
teaspoon
textbook
themselves
thumbtack
toadstool
toothache
toothbrush
treetop
underground
underline
understand
underwear
upright
wallpaper
warehouse
washcloth
watchman
waterfall
watermelon
weekend
whatever
wheelbarrow
whenever
whirlwind
whoever

Count on summer.
Complete each sentence with information about summer.

One summer holiday is_____

Two summer sports are _____

Three summer months are_____

Four types of summer clothing are _____

_____

Five kinds of summer weather are _____

_____

Six things to do in the summer are _____

_____

Seven things you see in the summer are_____

_____

Eight words to describe summer are _____

_____

Nine things that keep you cool are _____

_____

Ten things that are as hot as summer are_____

_____

Copy the word numbers 1-10 below: _____

_____   _____   _____

_____   _____   _____

_____   _____   _____

Practice subtraction with a deck of cards.

Give your child the number cards in a deck.

Let them flip up two cards and then add the amounts together. Fill in the chart below with the sum they get. When they reach the top, the game ends.

1	2	3	4	5	6	7	8	9	10	11	12	13	14	15	16	17	18	19	20

Let's practice handwriting for the coming school year. Do your best in writing.

A

a

a

a

write three words that begins with the letter a

Similarity and differences
Fill in the following chart with similarities and differences about you and a sibling or a friend.

Differences in you	Similarities in both of you	Differences in friend

Practice subtraction with a deck of cards.
Give your child the number cards in a deck.
Let them flip up two cards and then add the amounts together. Fill in the chart below with the sum they get. When they reach the top, the game ends.

1	2	3	4	5	6	7	8	9	10	11	12	13	14	15	16	17	18	19	20

Let's practice handwriting for the coming school year. Do your best in writing.

B

b

B

b

write three words that begins with the letter b

Animal alphabet

Write an animal for each letter of the alphabet. You might have to be creative for the letters that is hard to come up with an animal. For ex: U-understanding dog

A_____   N_____

B_____   O_____

C_____   P_____

D_____   Q_____

E_____   R_____

F_____   S_____

G_____   T_____

H_____   U_____

I_____   V_____

J_____   W_____

K_____   X_____

L_____   Y_____

M_____   Z_____

If you had $4.00 to spend on food. What could you buy? Find the prices of the items below. Add the prices of the items below. Then tell if you have enough money to buy the food.

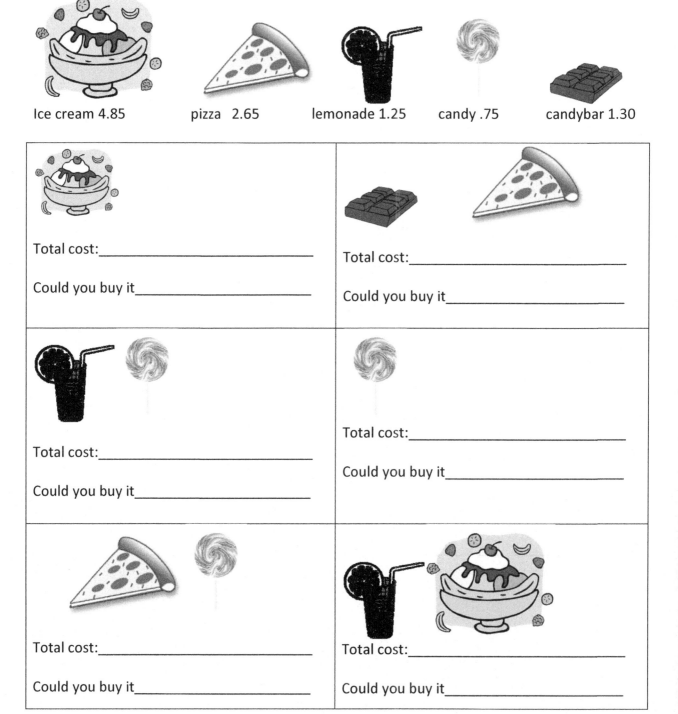

Ice cream 4.85   pizza   2.65   lemonade 1.25   candy .75   candybar 1.30

Total cost:_____

Could you buy it_____

Total cost:_____

Could you buy it_____

Total cost:_____

Could you buy it_____

Total cost:_____

Could you buy it_____

Total cost:_____

Could you buy it_____

Total cost:_____

Could you buy it_____

Let's practice handwriting for the coming school year. Do your best in writing.

C

c

C

c

write three words that begins with the letter c

Have your student fill in the following chart with a variety of syllable words. Have them write at least three of each, if they can do more, excellent.

One syllable word	Two syllable words
cat	happy

Three syllable words	Four syllable words
vacation	elevator

Add the numbers on each circle. Outline the circles using the color code below.

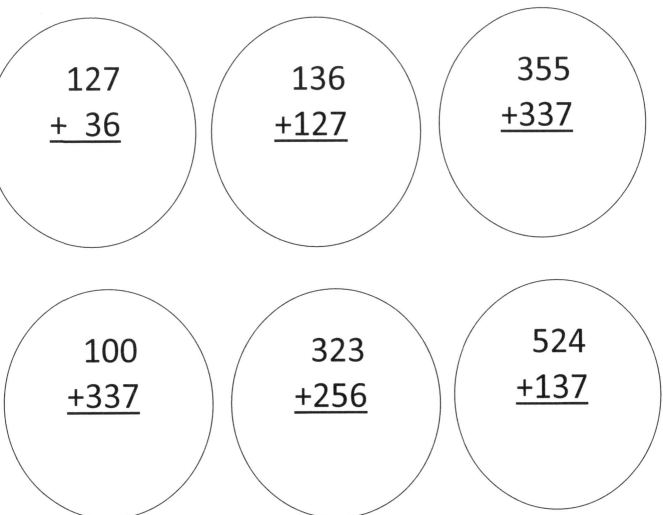

$$127 + 36$$

$$136 + 127$$

$$355 + 337$$

$$100 + 337$$

$$323 + 256$$

$$524 + 137$$

Yellow:100-200
Red:201-300
Blue: 301-400
Green:401-500
Purple:501-600
Orange:601-700

Let's practice handwriting for the coming school year. Do your best in writing.

D

d

$\mathcal{D}$

d

write three words that begins with the letter d

How many words can you create from the following words below:

Summer vacation

Draw the correct hands on the clock.

4:00

3:30

5:30

7:15

9:45

10:30

12:00

2:15

6:45

Let's practice handwriting for the coming school year. Do your best in writing.

E

e

$\mathcal{E}$

$\mathcal{e}$

write three words that begins with the letter e

Answer the following about why you are thankful. Write your answers in complete sentences. Complete sentences begin with a capital letter and end with a punctuation mark.

Who are you thankful for?_____

_____

What are you thankful for?_____

_____

Where are you thankful?_____

_____

When are you thankful?_____

_____

Why are you thankful?_____

_____

How do you show that you are thankful?_____

_____

Draw a picture to show one of your answers below.

Lets fill in the hundreds chart. Then color in all of the even numbers. Even numbers have pairs.

Let's practice handwriting for the coming school year. Do your best in writing.

F

f

$\mathcal{F}$

f

write three words that begins with the letter f

Punctuate the following sentences correctly. There will be periods, question marks, exclamation marks, and commas.

Rabbits have long ears short tails and long legs

What do your horses like to eat

Wow your dog is fast

What is the difference between a bunny rabbit and a hare

Are you going to feed your animals today

I like our cats dog and chickens

Hurry up the pigs are hungry

Did you get some cold water for them to drink

Do you like playing with my animals

Lets practice counting out loud. Have your student jump in place, step, clap their hands, or any other activity to get them moving.

Count by 2s up to 50

Count by 10s up to 150

Count by 5s up to 100

Count by 25's up to 200

Count backwards from 50 to 1

Count up to 200 by 1s

Let's practice handwriting for the coming school year. Do your best in writing.

G

g

$\mathcal{G}$

g

write three words that begins with the letter g

Let's punctuate the following. There are missing periods, question marks, exclamation marks, colons, and commas.

Do you want to play at the park swim at the beach or stay at home

July 4 2020

Honolulu Hawaii

Mr Gregory J Maryon

Let's go home and play with my toys

Hurry up or we will be late

I like to eat apples oranges and bananas

Is your cat climbing up that tree

Look at your cat climbing up the tree

Zirconia North Carolina

December 25 2019

4 00 p.m.

7 30 a m

Let's fill in the hundreds chart starting at 101

101									
									200

Let's practice handwriting for the coming school year. Do your best in writing.

H

h

$\mathcal{H}$

h

write three words that begins with the letter h

Circle the word in each row that is spelled incorrectly

chain	rain	clouds	rivir
chief	cheak	chase	dirt
change	shadow	coler	sunshine
poeple	pretty	girl	mom
man	dog	puppies	wintur
sumur	color	rainbow	bad
money	dimes	penny	nicel
pool	beach	watur	swim
dance	funny	frends	family
faith	chill	cange	charm

Turn your book sideways and fill in the boxes with:

- A star in the first box
- A circle in the third box
- A rectangle in the fifth box
- A heart in the second box
- A triangle in the fourth box
- A squiggly line in the sixth box
- The first letter in your name in the seventh box
- The first letter in your last name in the eighth box
- A smiley face in the tenth box
- A sad face in the ninth box

Let's practice handwriting for the coming school year. Do your best in writing.

I

i

$\mathcal{l}$

i

write three words that begins with the letter i

Personification is a way to describe something as though it were human. List three actions for each item. EX: wind---whisper, howl, race

sunlight_____

summer_____

tears_____

shadow_____

waterfall_____

river_____

clouds_____

rain_____

Use personification to write a sentence for each item.
Ex: The wind whispered through the tree branches.

sunlight_____

summer_____

tears_____

shadow_____

waterfall_____

river_____

clouds_____

rain_____

Practice three digit subtraction

$$874$$
$$-251$$

$$348$$
$$-138$$

Borrow from the neighbor on these:

$$743$$
$$-538$$

$$242$$
$$-113$$

$$888$$
$$-459$$

$$333$$
$$-207$$

Let's practice handwriting for the coming school year. Do your best in writing.

J

j

$\mathcal{J}$

i

write three words that begins with the letterj

Give your student some letter tiles or a pan with a little flour sprinkled inside of it. Let them spell the following words or write them in the flour with their finger.

Spell the numbers 1 through ten

Spell the color words: red, yellow, orange, blue, green, purple, brown, black, white

Have them write their name

Math facts out loud

Read the following math facts to your child out loud and have them answer. If they learn best by moving---have them clap their hands every time they answer. If they miss any, circle to work on it. Copy the ones that they miss and write them on an index card to continue practicing throughout the day.

0+3=3	0+4=4	0+5=5
1+3=4	1+4=5	1+5=6
2+3=5	2+4=6	2+5=7
3+3=6	3+4=7	3+5=8
4+3=7	4+4=8	4+5=9
5+3=8	5+4=9	5+5=10
6+3=9	6+4=10	6+5=11
7+3=10	7+4=11	7+5=12
8+3=11	8+4=12	8+5=13
9+3=12	9+4=13	9+5=14

Let's practice handwriting for the coming school year. Do your best in writing.

K

k

$\mathcal{K}$

k

write three words that begins with the letter k

Homophone pairs
Have students write a sentence that contains the two homophone pairs listed below.

Sunday/sundae

_____
- -
_____
_____
- -
_____

pear/pair

_____
- -
_____
_____
- -
_____

would/wood

_____
- -
_____
_____
- -
_____

see/sea

_____
- -
_____
_____
- -
_____

Follow the directions for coloring the eggs. Then write a fraction to answer each question.

Color two eggs pink and three eggs green What fraction of the eggs are pink_____	Color four eggs yellow and one egg red What fraction of the eggs are red_____
Color one egg blue and three eggs green What fraction of the eggs are blue_____	Color three eggs pink and four eggs purple What fraction of the eggs are pink_____
Color three eggs yellow and five eggs red What fraction of the eggs are yellow_____	Color two eggs blue and four eggs purple What fraction of the eggs are blue_____
Color six eggs orange and one egg pink What fraction of the eggs are pink_____	Color three eggs pink and two eggs yellow What fraction of the eggs are yellow_____

Let's practice handwriting for the coming school year. Do your best in writing.

L

l

L

l

write three words that begins with the letter l

Write a page about your Mom by completing the following:

If my mom were a flower, she would be a _____

because_____

If my mom were a song, she would be_____

because_____

If my mom were a super hero, she would be_____

because_____

If my mom were candy, she would be _____

because_____

If my mom were a car, she would be_____

because_____

If my mom were a color, she would be_____

because_____

If my mom were an animal, she would be_____

because_____

If my mom were a TV show, she would be_____

because_____

Math facts out loud

Read the following math facts to your child out loud and have them answer. If they learn best by moving---have them clap their hands every time they answer. If they miss any, circle to work on it. Copy the ones that they miss and write them on an index card to continue practicing throughout the week.

0+3=3	0+4=4	0+5=5
1+3=4	1+4=5	1+5=6
2+3=5	2+4=6	2+5=7
3+3=6	3+4=7	3+5=8
4+3=7	4+4=8	4+5=9
5+3=8	5+4=9	5+5=10
6+3=9	6+4=10	6+5=11
7+3=10	7+4=11	7+5=12
8+3=11	8+4=12	8+5=13
9+3=12	9+4=13	9+5=14

Let's practice handwriting for the coming school year. Do your best in writing.

M

m

m

m

write three words that begins with the letter m

Fill in the following chart

NOUNS	VERBS	ADJECTIVES	PRONOUNS

Math facts out loud

Read the following math facts to your child out loud and have them answer. If they learn best by moving---have them clap their hands every time they answer. If they miss any, circle to work on it. Copy the ones that they miss and write them on an index card to continue practicing throughout the week.

0+6=6	0+7=7	0+8=8
1+6=7	1+7=8	1+8=9
2+6=8	2+7=9	2+8=10
3+6=9	3+7=10	3+8=11
4+6=10	4+7=11	4+8=12
5+6=11	5+7=12	5+8=13
6+6=12	6+7=13	6+8=14
7+6=13	7+7=14	7+8=15
8+6=14	8+7=15	8+8=16
9+6=15	9+7=16	9+8=17

Let's practice handwriting for the coming school year. Do your best in writing.

N

n

n

n

write three words that begins with the letter n

Write the follow words on pieces of paper and place on the floor:

NOUNS   VERBS   ADJECTIVES   PRONOUNS

Call out the following to your child and have them correctly stand on the pages.

pretty
cow
jump
i
he
scared
girl
she
walked
train
we
tall
dog
you
short
pink
soft
house
street
me
him
eat
sat
run

Math facts out loud

Read the following math facts to your child out loud and have them answer. If they learn best by moving---have them clap their hands every time they answer. If they miss any, circle to work on it. Copy the ones that they miss and write them on an index card to continue practicing throughout the week.

0+6=6	0+7=7	0+8=8
1+6=7	1+7=8	1+8=9
2+6=8	2+7=9	2+8=10
3+6=9	3+7=10	3+8=11
4+6=10	4+7=11	4+8=12
5+6=11	5+7=12	5+8=13
6+6=12	6+7=13	6+8=14
7+6=13	7+7=14	7+8=15
8+6=14	8+7=15	8+8=16
9+6=15	9+7=16	9+8=17

Let's practice handwriting for the coming school year. Do your best in writing.

O

o

$\mathcal{O}$

$\mathcal{O}$

write three words that begins with the letter o

Grab socks and roll them into a ball. Get four containers and place a label in front of them. You are going to call out a variety of words and your student will throw the socks into the correct container. Label them noun, verbs, adjectives, and pronouns

boat
climb
clouds
drink
five
hair
hard
her
him
I
me
orange
pictures
rabbit
read
scratch
she
sleep
smile
sprint
them
thin
three
truck
ugly
us
water

Math facts out loud

Read the following math facts to your child out loud and have them answer. If they learn best by moving---have them clap their hands every time they answer. If they miss any, circle to work on it. Copy the ones that they miss and write them on an index card to continue practicing throughout the week.

0+9=9	0+10=10
1+9=10	1+10=11
2+9=11	2+10=12
3+9=12	3+10=13
4+9=13	4+10=14
5+9=14	5+10=15
6+9=15	6+10=16
7+9=16	7+10=17
8+9=17	8+10=18
9+9=18	9+10=19

Let's practice handwriting for the coming school year. Do your best in writing.

P

p

$\mathcal{P}$

p

write three words that begins with the letter p

Illustrate a picture of your pet. Then write a short story about your pet.

Math facts out loud

Read the following math facts to your child out loud and have them answer. If they learn best by moving---have them clap their hands every time they answer. If they miss any, circle to work on it. Copy the ones that they miss and write them on an index card to continue practicing throughout the week.

0+9=9	0+10=10
1+9=10	1+10=11
2+9=11	2+10=12
3+9=12	3+10=13
4+9=13	4+10=14
5+9=14	5+10=15
6+9=15	6+10=16
7+9=16	7+10=17
8+9=17	8+10=18
9+9=18	9+10=19

Let's practice handwriting for the coming school year. Do your best in writing.

Q

q

2

q

write three words that begins with the letter q

Use the following fragments and write a complete sentence for each.

fuzzy tails   down the bunny trail

_____

_____

_____

_____

_____

_____

long floppy ears   lazy dog howls

_____

_____

_____

_____

_____

_____

in the garden   a big juicy carrot

_____

_____

_____

_____

_____

_____

How many tens are in the following:

543 _____   789_____ 43_____ 89_____

2223_____   7654_____   80_____ 809_____

How many ones are in the following:

43 _____   6_____ 46_____ 4567_____

76 _____ 64_____   32_____ 80_____

How many hundreds are in the following:

423 _____   546_____   456_____   4657_____

765 _____   898_____   6544_____ 2000_____

Let's practice handwriting for the coming school year. Do your best in writing.

R

r

R

r

write three words that begins with the letter r

Look- discover, examine, gaze, glance, glimpse, notice, observe, peek, see, spy, study, view, watch.

The above is a list of synonyms for the word "look". Write a 3-4 sentence paragraph about what you saw when looking into the pond. Use a variety of words instead of the word "look." Then illustrate a picture about what you saw.

Adding with thousands.

4321	5432	7642	9080
+2100	+5432	+6541	+8021

Subtraction regrouping more than once

532	5678	7632	9722
-378	-4789	-2785	-4834

Let's practice handwriting for the coming school year. Do your best in writing.

S

s

$\mathcal{S}$

$\mathcal{s}$

write three words that begins with the letter s

ABC Order—number the following in the correct order 1-3.

girl gift give	sneak snow sniffle
rip ring ribbon	wrap write wreath
trim trunk tree	sled slush slippery
present promise prance	wish winter wide

2014
July

Sun	Mon	Tue	Wed	Thu	Fri	Sat
		1	2	3	4	5
6	7	8	9	10	11	12
13	14	15	16	17	18	19
20	21	22	23	24	25	26
27	28	29	30	31		

What is the 3rd Monday of the month?_____

What day is the 2nd Saturday of the month?_____

How many weeks are in a complete year?_____

How many days are in a year? Normally_____

If today was July 8, what will be in 10 days?_____

What is one week before July 16th?_____

Write all of the number days for Wednesday_____

Let's practice handwriting for the coming school year. Do your best in writing.

T

t

I

t

write three words that begins with the letter t

Working with abbreviations

Write your names initials _____

Write your teacher's initials _____

Write your state abbreviation_____

Do you know what ASAP stands for_____

Do you know what FYI stands for_____

Brainstorm with your student other common abbreviations that you know of. For example: UFO NBA   FBI

6 X1	2 X6	5 X2	1 X8	4 X2	3 X6	1 X2	2 X2	1 X1	6 X4
3 X5	1 X6	4 X6	3 X4	1 X0	3 X7	1 X10	4 X8	3 X2	5 X4
8 X2	6 X0	1 X9	3 X4	9 X2	5 X5	1 X5	7 X0	1 X2	6 X2
3 X1	5 X6	3 X3	3 X0	4 X0	3 X6	4 X4	3 X8	5 x10	3 X10
5 X9	5 X4	1 X7	7 X2	6 X6	5 X2	4 X2	7 X6	8 X6	8 X0
9 X6	5 X7	2 X0	5 X6	9 X4	0 X0	1 X4	1 X3	4 X7	10 X4
10 X2	5 X0	10 X6	5 X3	5 X8	5 X1	5 X0	0 X4	3 X2	3 X9

Let's practice handwriting for the coming school year. Do your best in writing.

U

u

𝓊

𝓊

write three words that begins with the letter u

Analogy—expresses relationship between two things. Teacher read these aloud and have your student answer them.

Scissors is to cut as broom is to?   SWEEP

Car is to mechanic as body is to

Black is to white as up is to

Kindness is to friend as cruelty is to

Snow is to winter as rain is to

Arm is to hand as leg is to

Tropical is to hot as polar is to

Poodle is to dog as eagle is to

Ring is to finger as necklace is to

Monday is to weekday as Saturday is to

Scissors are to cut as ruler is to

Green is to go as red is to

Carrot is to vegetable as peach is to

Worried is to calm as upset is to

Wolf is to pack as fish is to

Car is to road as boat is to

Sun is to day as moon is to

Play WAR addition.
Use a deck of cards and take out only the numbers.
You and a partner flip up two cards and add them together.

Whoever gets the higher sum, grabs the pile.

Let's practice handwriting for the coming school year. Do your best in writing.

V

V

$\mathcal{V}$

$\mathcal{v}$

write three words that begins with the letter v

Write the months of the year. Spell the entire word

Jan_____

Feb_____

M_____

A_____

M_____

J_____

J_____

Aug_____

Sept_____

Oct_____

Nov_____

Dec_____

Write me the days of the week

Sun_____Mon_____

Tues_____Wed_____

Thurs_____Fri_____

Sat_____

Teacher- today take out some food from your pantry and set on the table. Tape small pieces of paper and write money amounts on the food. Let your child practice "shopping" for some items and then adding them up. If you do just dollars, they can add up on paper. If you do cents as well, you can show them how to use a calculator.

You can give them a list of things that you want to purchase and let them add them up.

Let's practice handwriting for the coming school year. Do your best in writing.

W

W

$\mathcal{W}$

w

write three words that begins with the letter w

Up is to down as in is to _____

Minute is to hour as day is to _____

Month is to year as week is to _____

Over is to under as top is to _____

Big is to little as giant is to_____

Sound is to ear as sight is to _____

Page is to book as word is to _____

Wood is to tree as water is to _____

Hive is to bee as doghouse is to _____

Up is to down as right is to _____

Lamb is to sheep as kitten is to _____

Big is to little as large is to _____

Black is to white as dark is to _____

Day is to night as morning is to _____

Knee is to leg as elbow is to _____

Chicken is to farm as monkey is to _____

Fork is to spoon as glass is to _____

Wing is to bird as fin is to _____

Feather is to duck as fur is to _____

East is to west as north is to _____

1. I bought a ball for $2.42, and a bat for $1.75. How much did I spend in all?

2. I went out to lunch and spent $2.75 on pizza, 43¢ on an apple, and 85¢ on milk. How much did I spend in all?

3. I ran 7 miles on Monday, 3 on Tuesday, 12 on Wednesday, 1 on Thursday, and 8 on Friday. How many miles did I run all week?

4. My plants grew 2 " last month, 3" this month, and I expect they will grow 1 ½ more inches in the coming months. How tall will my plants be?

5. My girls weight 23 lbs, 57 lbs, and 76 lbs. How many lbs all together do they weigh?

Let's practice handwriting for the coming school year. Do your best in writing.

X

X

$\mathcal{X}$

$\mathcal{x}$

write three words that begins with the letter x

Synonyms for Super Dad

| intelligent | construct | stream | great | correct | repair |
| forest | glad | chef | grin | | |

Read each sentence. Use words from the box that are synonyms for the bold faced words. Write the synonyms on the lines.

My dad is a **wonderful** guy!_____

Just thinking of him makes me **smile**._____

He is always **happy** to spend time with me._____

Sometimes we go fishing at the **creek.**_____

Other times we camp out in the **woods.**_____

My dad showed me how to **build** a birdhouse._____

He also taught me how to **fix** a flat tire on my bike._____

Dad is also a very good **cook.**_____

I think my dad is very **smart.**_____

When I ask him a question, he always knows the **right** answer._____

_____

6 X1	2 X6	5 X2	1 X8	4 X2	3 X6	1 X2	2 X2	1 X1	6 X4
3 X5	1 X6	4 X6	3 X4	1 X0	3 X7	1 X10	4 X8	3 X2	5 X4
8 X2	6 X0	1 X9	3 X4	9 X2	5 X5	1 X5	7 X0	1 X2	6 X2
3 X1	5 X6	3 X3	3 X0	4 X0	3 X6	4 X4	3 X8	5 x10	3 X10
5 X9	5 X4	1 X7	7 X2	6 X6	5 X2	4 X2	7 X6	8 X6	8 X0
9 X6	5 X7	2 X0	5 X6	9 X4	0 X0	1 X4	1 X3	4 X7	10 X4
10 X2	5 X0	10 X6	5 X3	5 X8	5 X1	5 X0	0 X4	3 X2	3 X9

Color the border of the ones that you do not know and copy them onto a card to memorize today.

Let's practice handwriting for the coming school year. Do your best in writing.

Y

y

𝒴

𝓎

write three words that begins with the letter y

Teachers place some objects on the table and ask your child to give you 3 facts about each item and one opinion.

Use a highlighter to color in the number being rounded.
Rounding to the nearest ten:

56_____   31_____   18_____   43_____

12_____   27_____   35_____   67_____

Rounding to the nearest hundred

463_____   654_____   266_____   615_____

875_____   327_____   878_____   101_____

Round to the nearest thousand

6536_____   7437_____   8764_____   9008_____

9432_____   1121_____   3522_____   8444_____

Let's practice handwriting for the coming school year. Do your best in writing.

Z

z

$\mathcal{Z}$

$\mathcal{z}$

write three words that begins with the letter z

Memory helps

Teacher place a bunch of items on the table in front of your student. You can try ten items and see how they do.

Let your child look at the items for a few moments, then instruct them to close their eyes . You remove one item from the pile and see if they can remember which object was removed.

You can play this multiple times with more objects. Crayons, food items, books, etc can be used.

6 X1	2 X6	5 X2	1 X8	4 X2	3 X6	1 X2	2 X2	1 X1	6 X4
3 X5	1 X6	4 X6	3 X4	1 X0	3 X7	1 X10	4 X8	3 X2	5 X4
8 X2	6 X0	1 X9	3 X4	9 X2	5 X5	1 X5	7 X0	1 X2	6 X2
3 X1	5 X6	3 X3	3 X0	4 X0	3 X6	4 X4	3 X8	5 x10	3 X10
5 X9	5 X4	1 X7	7 X2	6 X6	5 X2	4 X2	7 X6	8 X6	8 X0
9 X6	5 X7	2 X0	5 X6	9 X4	0 X0	1 X4	1 X3	4 X7	10 X4
10 X2	5 X0	10 X6	5 X3	5 X8	5 X1	5 X0	0 X4	3 X2	3 X9

Practice writing your name in print and in cursive

Write your pets name in print and in cursive

Write your favorite color in print and in cursive

Grab a marker and color in the letters in the following sentences that should be capitalized.

johnny appleseed was born on september 26, 1774.

his real name was john chapman.

he traveled through ohio and indiana planting apple orchards.

there are many story's about johnny's adventures.

some say he wore a pot on his head instead of a hat.

some claim johnny never wore shoes, summer or winter.

none of these stories about johnny have been proven true.

until his death in 1845, he kept traveling and planting apple trees.

```
  196        543        486
+328        +48       +235
```

```
  182        559        256
 +98       +176       + 155
```

```
  348        536        754
 +99        +87        +  9
```

Write a word that describes the following phrases. For example: bell---clang.

a balloon bursting_____

a rusty hinge_____

a horse walking_____

a firecracker_____

ocean waves_____

falling rain_____

a candy wrapper_____

stepping in mud_____

a banjo string_____

a happy cat_____

a noisy dog_____

What is your favorite ice cream treat? Draw a picture of it and write 3-4 sentences describing the treat.

Play WAR addition with a friend like you did before.

Flip up two cards each and add them together. Higher number takes the pile.

List me 3 things that are small:

_____

_____

_____

List me 3 things that are soft:

_____

_____

_____

List me 3 parts of your body:

_____

_____

_____

List me 3 things that are red

_____

_____

_____

List me three things that can roll

_____

_____

_____

Write a letter to a friend telling them about what sort of summer you are having.

_____

_____

_____

_____

Let's practice some multiplication facts out loud. Have your child jump, take a step, clap their hands every time they answer correctly.

0x1=0	1x1=1	2x2=4
0x2=0	1x2=2	2x3=6
0x3=0	1x3=3	2x4=8
0x4=0	1x4=4	2x5=10
0x5=0	1x5=5	2x6=12
0x6=0	1x6=6	2x7=14
0x7=0	1x7=7	2x8=16
0x8=0	1x8=8	2x9=18
0x9=0	1x9=9	

These should be fairly easy, if not highlight them and continue working on them today.

Circle the word that is spelled incorrectly in each row

rag	crash	behst	half	matter
went	hand	stand	thomp	past
rawcks	lunch	fish	pond	jump
screme	raise	seat	grade	gain
pail	pipe	mule	wise	scate
hog	crop	grannd	honest	caught
bet	tent	held	else	paast
sat	felt	last	send	soks

Write the plural for the following words. Remember if it ends in ch, sh, x, s, add "es"

Singular	Plural
boy	
box	
couch	
tree	
flower	
lunch	
class	
fox	
girl	
light	
table	
dress	

Let's practice some multiplication facts out loud. Have your child jump, take a step, clap their hands every time they answer correctly.

0x1=0	1x1=1	2x2=4
0x2=0	1x2=2	2x3=6
0x3=0	1x3=3	2x4=8
0x4=0	1x4=4	2x5=10
0x5=0	1x5=5	2x6=12
0x6=0	1x6=6	2x7=14
0x7=0	1x7=7	2x8=16
0x8=0	1x8=8	2x9=18
0x9=0	1x9=9	

These should be fairly easy, if not highlight them and continue working on them today.

Irregular plurals

I have one:	I have more than one:
mouse	
tooth	
man	
woman	
foot	
goose	
child	
fish	

Imagine taking a trip to the ocean. What would you see? What would you do?
What would you eat? Illustrate a picture and write 4-5 sentences about it.

Let's practice some multiplication facts out loud. Have your child jump, take a step, clap their hands every time they answer correctly.

3x3=9	5x4=20
3x4=12	5x5=25
3x5=15	5x6=30
3x6=18	5x7=35
3x7=21	5x8=40
3x8=24	5x9=45
3x9=27	

If you noticed it is not the complete set, but you have already gone over the other problems in the previous days. Remember to teach your student that it doesn't matter if you switch the numbers. 3x2 is the same as 2x3. Knowing this, they will look at the problems and realize that there are not as many to learn as it looks.

Circle the word in each group that is spelled incorrectly

shot	chance	match	watch	spaece
fense	such	crash	chew	batch
sharp	speech	ranje	chance	match
watch	showed	sock	priec	crash
such	batch	space	stage	hitcked
price	polic	office	engine	badge
excite	force	range	giner	giraffe
wird	showed	pushed	police	car

Big- colossal, enormous, gigantic, great, huge, large, mammoth, tall, tremendous.

By using the above synonyms for the word "big" I want you to imagine what it would be like to come across a dinosaur. Write a paragraph describe what it would be like. Use the above words in your sentences.

Let's practice some multiplication facts out loud. Have your child jump, take a step, clap their hands every time they answer correctly.

3x3=9	5x4=20
3x4=12	5x5=25
3x5=15	5x6=30
3x6=18	5x7=35
3x7=21	5x8=40
3x8=24	5x9=45
3x9=27	

If you noticed it is not the complete set, but you have already gone over the other problems in the previous days. Remember to teach your student that it doesn't matter if you switch the numbers. 3x2 is the same as 2x3. Knowing this, they will look at the problems and realize that there are not as many to learn as it looks.

You choose a topic sentence below.

Ice cream is the best dessert ever invented.

Cats are the best pets.

Summer is the best time of year.

(or your own ideas)

Now begin your paragraph with your topic sentence. Then add 3 sentences that "support" your topic sentence. All the sentences will have something in common with your first sentence.

Topic sentence:

_____
_____
_____
_____
_____

Sentences that support the topic sentence.

_____
_____
_____
_____
_____
_____
_____
_____
_____
_____
_____
_____

What are some things that you look forward to seeing or doing in the winter time? Draw a picture and write a bunch of words saying what you will enjoy. They don't have to be sentences, just fragments. For ex: ice skating, snow sledding, snow, hot cocoa, etc

Let's practice some multiplication facts out loud. Have your child jump, take a step, clap their hands every time they answer correctly.

3x3=9	5x4=20
3x4=12	5x5=25
3x5=15	5x6=30
3x6=18	5x7=35
3x7=21	5x8=40
3x8=24	5x9=45
3x9=27	

If you noticed it is not the complete set, but you have already gone over the other problems in the previous days. Remember to teach your student that it doesn't matter if you switch the numbers. 3x2 is the same as 2x3. Knowing this, they will look at the problems and realize that there are not as many to learn as it looks.

How many months are there in one year?_____

Name all of the months to your teacher………………………………..

What number month is your birthday?_____

How many days of the week are there?_____

Write the days of the
week?_____,_____,

_____,_____

_____,_____

_____,_____

Name me a month that spring occurs?_____

Name me a month that winter occurs?_____

Name me a month when summer occurs?_____

Name me a month when falls occurs?_____

What day was it yesterday?_____

What day is it tomorrow?_____

What day do we go to church on?_____

What day does the weekend begin on?_____

When is your birthday?_____

What is todays date—the month, day, and year?_____

What year is it?_____

What year were you born in?_____

Let's fill in the hundreds chart starting at 101

101									

Let's practice some multiplication facts out loud. Have your child jump, take a step, clap their hands every time they answer correctly.

3x3=9   5x4=20

3x4=12   5x5=25

3x5=15   5x6=30

3x6=18   5x7=35

3x7=21   5x8=40

3x8=24   5x9=45

3x9=27

If you noticed it is not the complete set, but you have already gone over the other problems in the previous days. Remember to teach your student that it doesn't matter if you switch the numbers. 3x2 is the same as 2x3. Knowing this, they will look at the problems and realize that there are not as many to learn as it looks.

Think of a chapter book that you have read aloud or alone. Fill in the following chart.

Title:_____

Author:_____

Fill in the chart with details that happened:

Beginning	Middle	End

Write a sentence using the homophones correctly:

To_____

Two_____

Too_____

Your_____

You're_____

There_____

Their_____

They're_____

Its_____

It's_____

Let's practice some multiplication facts out loud. Have your child jump, take a step, clap their hands every time they answer correctly.

3x3=9	5x4=20
3x4=12	5x5=25
3x5=15	5x6=30
3x6=18	5x7=35
3x7=21	5x8=40
3x8=24	5x9=45
3x9=27	

If you noticed it is not the complete set, but you have already gone over the other problems in the previous days. Remember to teach your student that it doesn't matter if you switch the numbers. 3x2 is the same as 2x3. Knowing this, they will look at the problems and realize that there are not as many to learn as it looks.

Grab a handful of change and let your child place the correct amount on the squares.

28 ¢	51¢	17¢
39¢	99¢	25¢
75¢	78¢	40¢

Write your own story with a topic sentence, at least two middle sentences and an ending sentence. Use your own idea or use one of these story starters.

The Best Day I Ever Had

My First Pet

I Was So Unhappy I Cried

If I Could Do Anything

Why I Like Myself

Title:

_____

Topic sentence:

_____

_____

Middle sentences:

_____

_____

_____

_____

Ending sentence (to sum it all up):

_____

_____

Let's practice some multiplication facts out loud. Have your child jump, take a step, clap their hands every time they answer correctly.

3x3=9	5x4=20
3x4=12	5x5=25
3x5=15	5x6=30
3x6=18	5x7=35
3x7=21	5x8=40
3x8=24	5x9=45
3x9=27	

If you noticed it is not the complete set, but you have already gone over the other problems in the previous days. Remember to teach your student that it doesn't matter if you switch the numbers. 3x2 is the same as 2x3. Knowing this, they will look at the problems and realize that there are not as many to learn as it looks.

Last day to practice these. The ones your student does not know, copy them onto index cards and continue to review them.

Answer the following in cursive writing.

What is your favorite color:

_____

_____

What is your favorite animal:

_____

_____

Write your full name:

_____

_____

What state do you live in:

_____

_____

Who is your favorite friend:

_____

_____

What activity do you like to do:

_____

_____

Say: advise, announce, command, declare, discuss, explain, instruct, mumble, mutter, notify, order, roar, sigh, speak, state, tell, vow, whine, whisper, yell

Using the above synonyms for the word "say" dictate a how to paragraph explaining how you expect the choir to perform at the annual school program. Every time you use the words above, cross them off.

Let's practice some multiplication facts out loud. Have your child jump, take a step, clap their hands every time they answer correctly.

4x4=16   6x6=36

4x6=24   6x7=42

4x7=28   6x8=48

4x8=32   6x9=54

4x9=36

If you noticed it is not the complete set, but you have already gone over the other problems in the previous days. Remember to teach your student that it doesn't matter if you switch the numbers. 3x2 is the same as 2x3. Knowing this, they will look at the problems and realize that there are not as many to learn as it looks.

Circle the correctly spelled word.

1. Would you like to travel into outer _____
   a. space
   b. spas
   c. spase
2. He used a _____ to draw the rocket.
   a. pensil
   b. pencel
   c. pencil
3. Where is the _____ station?
   a. polise
   b. police
   c. poleece
4. We saw _____ waves on the ocean.
   a. huje
   b. huege
   c. huge
5. A strong wind can _____ small boats.
   a. destroy
   b. destroi
   c. distroy
6. Ted was _____ on his birthday.
   a. joiyful
   b. joyful
   c. joiful
7. Don't _____ the surprise!
   a. spoil
   b. spoyl
   c. spiol
8. The new company will _____ fifty people.
   a. imploy
   b. emploi
   c. employ
9. She is _____ to her family and friends.
   a. loyal
   b. loiyl
   c. loil
10. Please lower your _____.
    a. voyc
    b. vois
    c. voice

Choose the correct word.

My family is planning a trip to (Knew, New) York State.

We each get to pick (one, won) place to visit.

My mom (once, wants) to go see the State of Liberty.

It stands (in, inn) New York Harbor.

My dad wants (to, two) visit the Guggenheim Museum.

(Its, It's) a famous building designed by Frank Lloyd Wright.

Of course, the museum has lots of great art, (to, too).

My sister has (read, red) books about Harriet Tubman.

She wants to go (sea, see) Harriet Tubman's home in Auburn.

And me, (wear, where) do I want to go?

I thought it over (for, four) a long time.

I (would, wood) like to see Niagara Falls.

It is on the (boarder, border) between New York and Canada.

I (know, no) this will be a wonderful vacation.

Let's practice some multiplication facts out loud. Have your child jump, take a step, clap their hands every time they answer correctly.

4x4=16   6x6=36

4x6=24   6x7=42

4x7=28   6x8=48

4x8=32   6x9=54

4x9=36

If you noticed it is not the complete set, but you have already gone over the other problems in the previous days. Remember to teach your student that it doesn't matter if you switch the numbers. 3x2 is the same as 2x3. Knowing this, they will look at the problems and realize that there are not as many to learn as it looks.

Write me a paragraph about what you look forward to doing this fall

Title:

_____

Topic sentence:

_____

3 sentences to support the topic sentence.

_____

_____

_____

_____

_____

_____

_____

_____

_____

Ending sentence to sum up your paragraph.

_____

_____

Do you remember how to abbreviate? I want you to write all of the days of the week and write abbreviations for them as well.

Use cursive writing

Let's practice some multiplication facts out loud. Have your child jump, take a step, clap their hands every time they answer correctly.

4x4=16   6x6=36

4x6=24   6x7=42

4x7=28   6x8=48

4x8=32   6x9=54

4x9=36

If you noticed it is not the complete set, but you have already gone over the other problems in the previous days. Remember to teach your student that it doesn't matter if you switch the numbers. 3x2 is the same as 2x3. Knowing this, they will look at the problems and realize that there are not as many to learn as it looks.

Fill in the following chart

Adjectives to describe the day today	Adjectives to describe you	Adjectives to describe ice cream

Here is a list of words that your 3rd grader should know how to read. Have them read down the list, jump every time they say a word, or throw a jelly bean into a container for every word they say correctly. Highlight any words they miss and copy them on index cards to go over again.

about
better
bring
carry
clean
cut
done
draw
drink
eight
fall
far
full
got
grow
hold
hot
hurt
if
keep
kind

Let's practice multiplying BINGO
Grab two dice and roll them. Multiply the two numbers and when you get an answer, color in
the squares below.

3	15	10	24	1
30	4	2	5	18
5	6	FREE	16	12
30	20	25	36	12
6	9	4	8	6

party   monkey   ice cream   pool   funny

Use the above words and construct a story about something that happened. Your story must be _____ sentences long. Teachers give an amount based upon your child's skill level.

Here is a list of words that your 3rd grader should know how to read. Have them read down the list, jump every time they say a word, or throw a jelly bean into a container for every word they say correctly. Highlight any words they miss and copy them on index cards to go over again.

laugh
light
long
much
myself
never
only
own
pick
seven
shall
show
six
small
start
ten
today
together
try
warm

Let's practice multiplying BINGO

Grab two dice and roll them. Multiply the two numbers and when you get an answer, color in the squares below.

25	15	30	20	15
20	36	12	24	5
18	9	FREE	24	18
4	12	3	12	6
8	12	30	6	4

mountain　　　water　　　　　thirsty　　　　purple　　　car

Use the above words and construct a story about something that happened. Your story must be _____sentences long. Teachers give an amount based upon your child's skill level.

Here is a list of words that your 3rd grader should know how to read. Have them read down the list, jump every time they say a word, or throw a jelly bean into a container for every word they say correctly. Highlight any words they miss and copy them on index cards to go over again.

apple
baby
back
ball
bear
bed
bell
bird
birthday
boat
box
boy
bread
brother
cake
car
cat
chair
chicken
children
Christmas
coat
corn
cow

Let's practice some multiplication facts out loud. Have your child jump, take a step, clap their hands every time they answer correctly.

7x7=49

7x8=56

7x9=63

8x8=64

8x9=72

9x9=81

This is the last of the basic math facts 1-9. Copy and work on memorizing them for this next year's school. Copy them onto index cards and work on memorizing them. Do one a day if it is hard.

Fill in the following sunshine with things that you cannot imagine life without. Then color in the the different sections with a variety of colors.

I
can't
IMAGINE
life
without…

Here is a list of words that your 3rd grader should know how to read. Have them read down the list, jump every time they say a word, or throw a jelly bean into a container for every word they say correctly. Highlight any words they miss and copy them on index cards to go over again.

day
dog
doll
door
duck
egg
eye
farm
farmer
father
feet
fire
fish
floor
flower
game
garden
girl
goodbye
grass
ground
hand
head
hill

Let's practice some multiplication facts out loud. Have your child jump, take a step, clap their hands every time they answer correctly.

7x7=49

7x8=56

7x9=63

8x8=64

8x9=72

9x9=81

This is the last of the basic math facts 1-9. Copy and work on memorizing them for this next year's school. Copy them onto index cards and work on memorizing them. Do one a day if it is hard.

List ten ways that I can show kindness to someone else:

KINDNESS

1 _____

2 _____

3 _____

4 _____

5 _____

6 _____

7 _____

8 _____

9 _____

10 _____

Here is a list of words that your 3rd grader should know how to read. Have them read down the list, jump every time they say a word, or throw a jelly bean into a container for every word they say correctly. Highlight any words they miss and copy them on index cards to go over again.

home
horse
house
kitty
leg
letter
man
men
milk
money
morning
mother
name
nest
night
paper
party
picture
pig
rabbit
rain
ring
robin

Multiplication facts 0s, 1s, 2s, 3s, 4s, 5s. Teacher, color in the squares they missed and work on them.

4 x0	3 x 2	5 x 1	4 x 5	2 x 0	1 x 8	7 x 2	1 x1
5 x2	4 x0	2 x8	1 x 4	7 x 5	3 x3	8 x 5	0 x5
8 x1	6 x5	9 x0	2 x4	0 x1	4 x2	1 x6	9 x2
3 x7	3 x5	4 x3	4 x1	2 x2	8 x0	5 x9	1 x2
5 x4	1 x7	0 x0	8 x2	5 x8	5 x6	3 x0	9 x1
5 x3	0 x4	6 x4	9 x 5	5 x0	4 x4	4 x8	0 x9
6 x0	7 x3	2 x3	4 x5	3 x6	9 x3	7 x 4	5 x3
3 x3	9 x3	0 x7	3 x2	4 x3	7 x4	3 x5	8 x3
4 x7	6 x2	4 x4	9 x3	1 x4	4 x9	1 x0	5 x4
0 x2	1 x9	3 x1	4 x7	3 x1	1 x5	2 x4	8 x4
1 x4	2 x1	4 x4	2 x7	0 x7	5 x7	2 x5	4 x9

Create a flip book for your student.

To make a booklet, stack three, 8 ½"x11" sheets of white paper and hold the pages vertically in front of you. Slide the top sheet upward one inch; then repeat the process for the second sheet. Next fold the paper thicknesses forward to create six graduated layers or pages. Staple close to the fold.

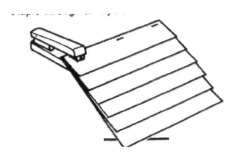

Have your child create their own story.

Write on each page things that your student enjoyed doing this summer. Label the story...My summer vacation on the top page.

Illustrate and add correctly written sentences.

Here is a list of words that your 3rd grader should know how to read. Have them read down the list, jump every time they say a word, or throw a jelly bean into a container for every word they say correctly. Highlight any words they miss and copy them on index cards to go over again.

school
seed
sheep
shoe
sister
snow
song
squirrel
stick
street
sun
table
thing
time
top
toy
tree
watch
water
way
wind
window
wood

Multiplication facts 0s, 1s, 2s, 3s, 4s, 5s 6s. Teachers color in the squares that your student misses.

4 x0	3 x 2	6 x 1	4 x 5	2 x 0	1 x 8	7 x 2	1 x1
5 x2	4 x0	2 x6	1 x 4	7 x 5	3 x6	8 x 5	0 x5
8 x1	6 x5	9 x0	2 x4	0 x1	4 x2	1 x6	9 x2
3 x7	3 x5	6 x3	4 x6	2 x2	8 x0	5 x9	1 x2
5 x4	1 x7	0 x0	8 x2	5 x8	5 x6	3 x0	9 x1
5 x3	0 x4	6 x4	9 x 5	5 x0	4 x4	4 x8	0 x9
6 x0	7 x3	2 x3	6 x5	3 x6	9 x3	7 x 4	5 x3
3 x3	9 x3	0 x7	3 x2	4 x3	7 x4	3 x5	8 x3
4 x7	6 x2	4 x4	9 x3	1 x6	4 x9	6 x6	5 x4
0 x2	6 x7	3 x1	4 x7	3 x1	1 x5	2 x4	8 x4
6 x9	2 x1	4 x4	6 x7	0 x7	5 x7	2 x5	6 x9

Circle one item in each category and construct a story based on those you chose.

CHARACTER	SETTING	PLOT
SMARTY MARTY	AT THE PARK	MAKING POPCORN
DANCING DAWN	ON AN ISLAND	MAKING BALLOON ANIMALS
ROBOT	AT THE GROCERY STORE	FIND WOLF TRACKS

Here is a list of words that your 3rd grader should know how to read. Have them read down the list, jump every time they say a word, or throw a jelly bean into a container for every word they say correctly. Highlight any words they miss and copy them on index cards to go over again.

high
every
near
add
food
between
own
below
country
plant
last
school
father
keep
tree
never
start
city
earth
eyes
light
thought
head
under
story

Multiplication facts 0-7. Teachers highlight the ones your student does not know.

4 x0	3 x 2	6 x 7	4 x 5	2 x 0	1 x 8	7 x 2	1 x1
5 x2	4 x0	2 x6	5 x 7	7 x 5	3 x6	8 x 5	0 x5
8 x1	6 x5	9 x0	2 x4	0 x1	4 x2	1 x6	9 x2
3 x7	3 x5	6 x3	4 x6	2 x2	8 x0	5 x9	1 x2
5 x4	1 x7	7 x7	8 x2	5 x8	5 x6	3 x0	9 x1
5 x3	7 x4	6 x4	9 x 5	5 x0	4 x4	4 x8	7 x9
6 x0	7 x3	2 x3	6 x5	3 x6	9 x3	7 x 4	5 x3
3 x3	9 x3	0 x7	3 x2	4 x3	7 x4	3 x5	8 x3
4 x7	6 x2	4 x4	9 x3	1 x6	4 x9	6 x6	5 x4
8 x7	6 x7	3 x1	4 x7	3 x1	7 x5	2 x4	8 x4
6 x9	2 x1	4 x4	6 x7	4 x7	5 x7	2 x5	6 x9

Create a flip book for your student.

To make a booklet, stack three, 8 ½"x11" sheets of white paper and hold the pages vertically in front of you. Slide the top sheet upward one inch; then repeat the process for the second sheet. Next fold the paper thicknesses forward to create six graduated layers or pages. Staple close to the fold.

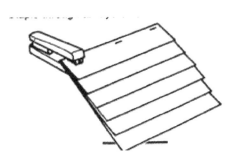

On each page write the following:

NOUNS

PROPER NOUNS

SINGULAR NOUNS

PLURAL NOUNS

VERBS

ADJECTIVES

Here is a list of words that your 3rd grader should know how to read. Have them read down the list, jump every time they say a word, or throw a jelly bean into a container for every word they say correctly. Highlight any words they miss and copy them on index cards to go over again.

saw
left
don't
few
while
along
might
close
something
seem
next
hard
open
example
begin
life
always
those
both
paper
together
got
group
often
run

Multiplication 1-8. Teachers highlight the ones that your student misses.

4 x0	3 x 2	6 x 7	8 x2	4 x 5	2 x 0	1 x 8	7 x 2	1 x1
5 x2	4 x0	3 x8	2 x6	5 x 7	7 x 5	3 x6	8 x 5	0 x5
8 x1	6 x5	9 x0	8 x4	2 x4	0 x1	4 x2	1 x6	9 x2
3 x7	3 x5	6 x3	1 x7	4 x6	2 x2	8 x0	5 x9	1 x2
5 x4	8 x3	7 x7	8 x5	8 x2	5 x8	5 x6	3 x0	9 x1
5 x3	7 x4	6 x4	9 x3	9 x 5	5 x0	4 x4	4 x8	7 x9
6 x0	7 x3	2 x3	7 x8	6 x5	3 x6	6 x8	7 x 4	5 x3
3 x3	9 x3	0 x7	6 x6	3 x2	4 x3	7 x4	3 x5	8 x3
4 x7	6 x2	4 x4	9 x8	9 x3	1 x6	4 x9	8 x8	5 x4
8 x7	6 x7	3 x1	5 x7	4 x7	3 x1	7 x5	2 x4	8 x4
6 x9	2 x1	4 x4	8 x3	6 x7	4 x7	7 x8	2 x5	6 x9

211

Fill in the following with a how to get ready in the morning.

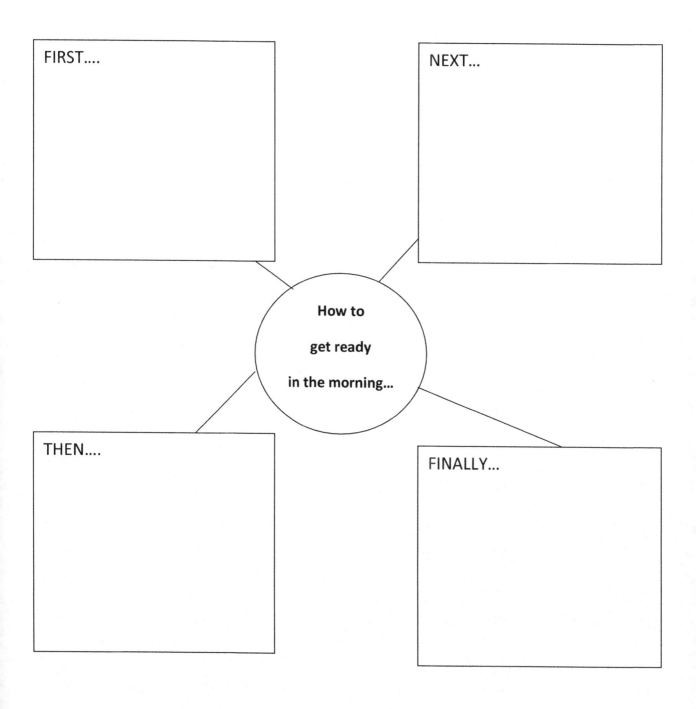

FIRST....

NEXT...

How to

get ready

in the morning...

THEN....

FINALLY...

Here is a list of words that your 3rd grader should know how to read. Have them read down the list, jump every time they say a word, or throw a jelly bean into a container for every word they say correctly. Highlight any words they miss and copy them on index cards to go over again.

important
until
children
side
feet
car
mile
night
walk
white
sea
began
grow
took
river
four
carry
state
once
book
hear
stop
without
second
late

100 Multiplication facts

9 x1	2 x2	5 x1	4 x3	0 x0	9 x9	3 x5	8 x5	2 x6	4 x7
5 x6	7 x5	3 x0	8 x8	1 x3	3 x4	5 x9	0 x2	7 x3	4 x1
2 x3	8 x6	0 x5	6 x1	3 x8	1 x1	9 x0	2 x8	6 x4	0 x7
7 x7	1 x4	6 x2	4 x5	2 x4	4 x9	7 x0	1 x2	8 x4	6 x5
3 x2	4 x6	1 x9	5 x7	8 x2	0 x8	4 x2	9 x8	3 x6	5 x5
8 x9	3 x7	9 x7	1 x7	6 x0	0 x3	7 x2	1 x5	7 x8	4 x0
8 x3	5 x2	0 x4	9 x5	6 x7	2 x7	6 x3	5 x4	1 x0	9 x2
7 x6	1 x8	9 x6	4 x4	5 x3	8 x1	3 x3	4 x8	9 x3	2 x0
8 x0	3 x1	6 x8	0 x9	8 x7	2 x9	9 x4	0 x1	7 x4	5 x8
0 x6	7 x1	2 x5	6 x9	3 x9	1 x6	5 x0	6 x6	2 x1	7 x9

Image that you were 20 feet tall!!! What would life be like? Illustrate and write a story about what life would be like.

Here is a list of words that your 3rd grader should know how to read. Have them read down the list, jump every time they say a word, or throw a jelly bean into a container for every word they say correctly. Highlight any words they miss and copy them on index cards to go over again.

miss

idea

enough

eat

face

watch

far

Indian

real

almost

let

above

girl

sometimes

mountains

cut

young

talk

soon

list

song

being

leave

family

it's

Made in the USA
Coppell, TX
25 May 2021